If the Largest Ship Could Feel Its Own Waves

If the Largest Ship Could Feel Its Own Waves

A Collection of Philosophical Poetry

By
ODA PUNKT

RESOURCE *Publications* • Eugene, Oregon

IF THE LARGEST SHIP COULD FEEL ITS OWN WAVES
A Collection of Philosophical Poetry

Copyright © 2022 Oda Punkt. All rights reserved. Except for brief quotations in critical publications or reviews, no part of this book may be reproduced in any manner without prior written permission from the publisher. Write: Permissions, Wipf and Stock Publishers, 199 W. 8th Ave., Suite 3, Eugene, OR 97401.

Resource Publications
An Imprint of Wipf and Stock Publishers
199 W. 8th Ave., Suite 3
Eugene, OR 97401

www.wipfandstock.com

PAPERBACK ISBN: 978-1-6667-5179-6
HARDCOVER ISBN: 978-1-6667-5180-2
EBOOK ISBN: 978-1-6667-5181-9

AUGUST 24, 2022 1:26 PM

To those who fought naked under a red sky

"Wake the water to remember me by"
—ODA PUNKT

Contents

Preface | xi

Acknowledgments | xiii

Part 1 · HALLWAY

Not Among Us | 3

Before the Storm | 4

Direction | 5

Dikaios | 6

A Dry World | 7

Risen | 12

Surface | 13

Slice | 14

Humanity Has the Morning | 15

Pillar | 16

Part 2 · FAMILY PORTRAIT

The Line | 19

Within It Sounds a Faded Song | 20

Vision | 21

The Dance | 22

Caretaker | 23

The Truth of Winter | 24

Prophetic Pop Songs | 26

Never | 28

Superiority | 30

Solid | 31

The Making of a Heartbreaker | 32

Black and White Meadow | 35

Part 3 · WARDROBE

All the Sunshine | 39

My Ancient Robes of Life | 40

Smoke and Mirrors | 41

Fortress of Memory | 42

Obstacle | 43

Sometimes | 44

Underground | 45

For Fucks Sake | 46

Before the Flaying | 47

Inversion | 48

Part 4 · WEDDING DRESS

The Waterlily and the Fishermen | 51

The Mountain | 52

Cinderella | 54

Edges | 55

Denial and Isolation | 58

The Unlikely Memories | 60

To Waste it All | 62

No Dogs in the Doorway | 65

Parasitical Symbiosis | 67

Seashell | 69

Tideless | 71

Undying | 74

Orange | 76

Part 5 · WHEN COLOR FOLDS

Corner Moon | 81

The Fold | 82

Bad Choices | 83

Black | 84

Snarvei | 85

Shortcut | 86

The Wave | 87

Promise | 89

Gullable | 90

Rope | 91

Part 6 · THE FIRST RIPPLE

My Funny Valentine | 95

Machine Gun Confusion | 96

What if the Clouds Are a Fog? | 97

Brand New Heaven | 98

No Title | 99

Point | 100

Vacation from Destiny | 101

Pinocchio | 102

Joke | 103

Light | 104

Fourth Dimension | 105

This is the first time you have been invited to my house. Before you come in, take a deep breath, and try to memorize the way out

Preface

LONG AGO I LEARNED the power of anti, the way that one extreme gives life to the opposite one-, and the-way emotion is built from the suppression of it.

I see political activists speak their minds, but every mind is filtered, and every word tailored to reach only those who already agree. With all the social rules imposed by each subculture, every individual is frozen, and the world is at a standstill.

There is a way to bring the tension of this paralysis into action. There is a way to transform the suppression of thought into freedom of speech.

I accept all realities as equal, and I am not here to tell you who to be. I am only here to encourage a reaction and a drive to break out of the constrictions placed upon you.

My poetry is intentionally representing suppressed opinions and realities, and therefore both politically incorrect and morally provoking. Through your reactions to my writings and my art, I hope you will arrive at yourself.

Acknowledgments

I WOULD LIKE TO THANK the following places for publishing the following poems:

"Cinderella," *The Dream Catcher* number 33, year 2016

"Orange," "The Making of a Heartbreaker," *STARK* number 2, year 2017

"The Mountain," *South Bank Poetry* number 31, April 2019

"Edges," *Artemis* number 22, May/June 2019

"All the sunshine," *Crosswinds Poetry* number 4, April/May 2019

"Anger," *The Journal* number 56 (by Sam Smith), year 2019

"Stalling," "All the sunshine," *The Seventh Quarry* number 31, Winter/Spring 2020

"Brand New Heaven," "What if the clouds are a fog?" "Machine Gun Confusion," "The Waterlily and the Fishermen," "Not Among Us," "Smoke and Mirrors," "Celebrity," "Black and White Meadow," *Neplanta*, year 2021

The name used for earlier publications is mostly Oda Dellagi. One publication is under Oda Waag, while the publications of 2021 are under Oda Punkt.

I would like to thank my great grandmother Dagny Gausåker who told me at the age of five that I should be a diplomat.

Acknowledgments

I would like to thank my elementary school teacher Elfrid Barth who told me at the age of eight to always sustain my strength.

I would like to thank my grandmother Liv Waag for showing me the true meaning of resilience.

If I had one advice to give it would be that both talent and intelligence are inferior to strength. Before focusing on your talents and knowledge, find something to live for, which you also would die for.

I would like to thank God for resurrecting me after I was in a coma, and for giving me new life many times over throughout my life.

I would like to thank Jesus for answering me with unconditional love when I prayed for punishment. My chains were already loose, but I lacked the will to free myself, until Jesus gave me will.

I would like to thank all individuals out there who refuse to conform to what is easy, and instead fight for what they believe in. Together, by the grace of God, we are doing the impossible.

Part 1
HALLWAY

NOT AMONG US

You wear a shirt that says
"ask me anything"
You take a sip of water
and stand next to the future

The future does not even
have a body
yet it has more than you
will ever have
The people, they flock to it

You climb the stage, and you sing
Every time you mess up the pitch
and forget the words, you get a nervous laugh
You look around the room

but no one noticed
"He had nothing to live for"
is what they say of you
as you are singing

BEFORE THE STORM

Stalling
long legs, short steps
cynical laughter
disappearing like
a ship
in a clear glass bottle

Someone who can
never see
anything but this zig zag outline
of my white sails
and forever body
wooden

and for everyday use
my untouched lips and my
windless heart
If you finally found me
I would not be a promise
I would be

a wordless being
with no cry for help
from no island
sailing
to nothing.

DIRECTION

If all winds lead here
I will turn yellow from pollen
All plants will take root in my sphere
No one can leave once fallen

If everything lands here
laying down, section upon section
no one will be able to glare
there will be no inspection

So let me instead be taken
split up and broken
drifting away in every direction
gone with the wind and the heavens

so that I can come to be
finally
something more than an illusion

DIKAIOS

Blank is my prison
Caught God in the act
Clouds are my reasons
The light is not white

The white only captures it
In the skies my anchor sits

Horse-colored purpose
Paroimia the truth
Time is the serpent
It swallows the youth

The white only captures it
In the skies my anchor sits

Autarkeia
Victoire de l'âme
Autarkeia
Rise from chaos

Autarkeia
Victoire de l'âme
Autarkeia
Dikaios, Dikaios, Dikaos

A DRY WORLD

I pet the cheek of the impossible
The large ballroom is filled with toxic crystals
They cut and distort eternity
Strange echoes
"Hello? Hello?" Ask the empty faces

They fervently demand to be crossed off
the to-do list
If only I had more red ink left
and I could pretend I cared
If only there was more blood left in the world

I let it go
the idea of pushing
a human life into their existence
The human body fights hard enough as it is
for the soul to also fight

In the past there was a different eternity
This ballroom was once an ocean
I pet their impossible desires
I pet the friction
pet the very annihilation of everything they are

Even though I've already been tortured to death
every second of my life
I will be the one to open the eyes of the world
so the world can see which eyes don't look back

There is no pain that you can experience now
to justify your sins

I inhale a bridal veil
I choke on your alleged innocence

Glassy eyes on the verge of tears
or eyes of glass, it does not matter
because you have always closed them

My ivory horse roars over the crowd
Down the stallion extends a white dress
The shadows of the rags are not soft as fabric
but hard as arrows

I descend on the pale adoring marble floor
The black stripes of the marble lead me to you
Remember that only the shadow
can travel faster than the speed of light
Into the past the light brings only darkness

By the dawn of time
God created the sea, the blood, the suffering, and the life
Then let it flow in, all the things you denied, one last time

Bird hearts stop to give me their freedom
trees are torn in half to break the seasons
and the world dries out

You hold your breath
because you know, it would have been better
if your heart didn't beat
if you could fly like them

Looking into your pointless eyelids was enough
to see you standing by my side
while I was tortured to death
Your denial was greater and stronger than my killer
but you never stopped my murder

For you, evil was far too great
even if your nothingness is infinitely greater

My horse kicks you in the head
You lose one of your ears into the dust
Now it gets wetter than it was
but red ink does not exist, it cannot be found here

No one can feel what nothing lost
No one can mourn what laziness loved
Once upon a time there was a time
to listen
You had ears that you never used

By the dawn of time
God created the sea, the blood, the suffering, and the life
Then let it flow in, all the things you denied, one last time

The sea extends into the ballroom
You throw empty containers outwards
but nothing floats on the waves of Hell
Your past is now your only destiny
Even Hell won't accept what never existed

The spotlights fight over the stage
It is unbearable to be torn between the sand and the spotlights
so hot, so cold, an enforced orgasm
the sand and floodlights, the sand, and the floodlights
It's so hard for you to accept that you've always been blind

You do not accept your judgment
The shadow sent you back in time
to the moments in which
you were always behind

Your empty containers are looking to find
the lost seconds

Your colorless blood
the waves of hell
the empty containers
Can you see your own glare in your own head?
Can you see the quotes on the pillowcases?

Can you hear the echo?
The repetitions from the textbooks?
In the depths of your own emptiness?
Can you see justice coming between life and yourself?

Can you see what's always beneath the surface?
What never needs to be erased because it never existed?
Nothing was worse than you
but you were nothing

Remember, love is the opposite of time
I gave you endless chances
and you chose infinity

The only thing that lights up under the floodlights
is my white horse of painstaking silk
on black clear hooves
Bird hearts are beating again
and the trees are gluing their stems

By the dawn of time
God created the sea, the blood, the suffering, and the life
Then let it flow in, all the things you denied, for the first time

Because this is only the beginning
It was up to me to find a future beyond your sin
but your sin was too great

No one ever felt hunger as much as you
and now you shall never stop swallowing your own flesh

I sing without inhaling
the tones are many
but cannot be counted in time
God lays me sideways once more

sideways as the first natural light
in the crack of the child opening his eyes
to a true morning.

RISEN

After my deaths I wake
Flowers drink me, and I drink them
My face moves the sky
I freeze the rain
not into ice
but into love

Hail grows large
like all compromises do
Can you stretch your breath
out through your fingertips
move it into a hurricane
rearrange the world
with your death?

No.

SURFACE

The suppressed murmurs
of the demonic wild
the fallen angel
stuck in a tree
cannot
be washed down

How many times
did I swallow
when in this coma?
the masculine bass
of the human heart

The loud screams of perfection
that still fallen angels have
Nothing is more unpleasant
than the sharpness of a vowel
How many times did it scratch the surface?

of my composure

SLICE

To summarize
the history of humankind

The first river after winter
smooth black truth

circleability
Steel cuts diamonds

the seam will open
where it was seamless

Behold, the paper cut galore

HUMANITY HAS THE MORNING

I am a flower field
blossoming on a dead branch
so massively beautiful
within meaninglessness

The shallow eternity
needs no salt to keep me afloat
I sink to the bottom
my face is still above the surface
alive in a dead world

The spotlight of the sky
is not like a pendulum
incapsulated in rusty metal
It swings back and forth
but then forth forever more
unleashed

The days are uncontrollable
Humanity has the morning
The sand is still warm from the sun
but you glow in artificial light
The freedom of choice

The eggs come out of the fridge
Birds are starting to hatch
The mornings are multiplied to eternity
the broken parts reflecting themselves
Freedom is swallowed
The picture is lost
So, I grow my unity greater than yours

hoping God will see me and not you

PILLAR

For every pillar I discover
the sky hangs even lower
They say it is a blessing
more ground to cover

My blood drips sideways
as the sky starts to bloom
I bend backwards
to walk into the living room.

Part 2
FAMILY PORTRAIT

THE LINE

I draw the line
down the river
around your eyes
things that only you know

You saw me waiting for hope
losing the years and the worlds
with a smile on my face
a straight line

WITHIN IT SOUNDS A FADED SONG

The powdered light
moving aimlessly yet true
the sequined dress
carefully tracing it

the stamina of the daughter
twirling her mother's hair
yet the mother does not
remember her lines

Like the sand on the ocean floor
keeps the shape of the waves
miles and miles above
the daughter believes

in what she never saw
a mysterious bright blue essence
that makes the breathing heavy
and the soap bubbles expand

As the poison spreads
throughout her limbs
something fades in the child
but it is not love

VISION

We reshaped the heart
so that we could find it everywhere
and now that lie is a good omen

THE DANCE

You place your trust
in the lies that suspend you
way above the ground
as if they were bonds that could tie
a family together

It feels like a darkening of the light
when you hang closer to the sun
with a rope around your neck
Down below, your children
they look up at you

Do not squirm nor bend
when your lies hold your being
Stay in their mercy
and never move
under the ceiling

The credit of your actions
goes to your children
Victory leads to misery
when your rewards are stolen

Time is the concept
the young ones do not know
and yet only they have it
To show

You place your trust
in the lies that suspend you
and although you cannot move
your lies can dance

CARETAKER

I am crossing the street slowly
at a red light
In my bare hands, I am holding a bird
I would die for, almost

The birds' lungs fall out of its mouth
It is protesting the song
Every corner of every house
demonstrates
that it all turns back to you

Home
could be where the birds have no wings
but it would not matter
because there is no higher place
than the rejection of death

There is no higher place
than in the middle of an embrace
in the middle of it all
Loving someone is
feeling they gave you eternal life

when your logic says they killed you
The rhythm of the dance is how we know
time always comes back
to this moment

THE TRUTH OF WINTER

Let me feel
the snowflakes fall heavy on my eyelids
Let me be seemingly sad
as if I once had something

It is a beautiful day
The spade against the concrete
sounds like church bells
There is no grave
underneath

Let it all go blurry and melt away
through artificial tears
Let it seem like an accident
like I was out of my element

Let me feel
for the first time ever
the truth of winter
Let me see
through the eyes that I closed

The summer is crystallized
into a vase of ice
yet the water overflows with emotions
as if my insides ever could
measure the world

Through your eyes
and their innocence
I break the winter
killing you
before you were born

Beautiful flowers
when all I ever did know
was how to keep decay
within a forever summer
All I ever did know
was how to not let go
of all that never mattered to me

Let me feel
for the first time ever
the truth of winter
Let me see
through the eyes that I closed

PROPHETIC POP SONGS

Through the church yard
by the fountain in the dark
I have the memory of running water
coming from this place
but it is winter
and I'm here

Show me those with white eyes
those without pupils
so that I can look at them
and they cannot
look at me
They'll be like a painting

show them to me
Only to walk into the white woods
that have no pathways
to walk outside of the map
and even beyond the piles of logs
and dead trees

that I killed previously
I am out of breath
They all grow up, and they
shoot up just to lean down
They are white just to
grow blackness

The hanging birch trees
in the winters
they make oxygen
just to love me

Oh, these kids, they
listen to prophetic pop songs

about how they are going to meet me
when they turn thirteen
They'll be like the empty frames
of paintings
Hang them for me
I will drown all the barking dogs

in a brand-new place
far from the stolen innocence
and the empty fountains
they witnessed
It appears I have been running
to get to this place

an opening in the sky
where I can gaze at the star-like
flying cigarettes in the air
and only here and only here
can I find them
although they are not

shooting stars
not the dream of a past
nor the hope of a future
and my life is nothing
but the memory of running water
in a fountain in a graveyard

that is
too dark to see

NEVER

I see the sky
in the dew of the forest leaves
but never above me

I feel the safety
of the ground beneath my feet
that my feet never touch

I hear my heart
beats in my head
That's not where the heart is

Every time I fall asleep
I jerk up, standing
I fall to my knees

If you look, you'll see
the hanging birch trees
giving it all away
giving it all away

Shockingly
fast pain in my heart
eternally
slow pain in my head
I pass out
and I am dead; I was dead

If you look, you'll see
the hanging birch trees
giving it all away
giving it all away

If you really look, you'll see what I mean
that this day
it was never

SUPERIORITY

Did you find the light of winter?
Did you lose the civilizations?
What are you building
now that building is a sin?

SOLID

There is nothing you hate more
than unrequited love
There is nothing more embarrassing
than being the bigger person

THE MAKING OF A HEARTBREAKER

Growing up, I had a room
full of things I found in the desert
a naked body, a dying tree
a grain of sand, a part of you
and still nothing at all

You have always been
so proud to be a mother
Now, with me, I bring to mankind
a spell to last forever
Without me, the sound of their eyelashes
as they opened and shut
were almost as good as heartbeats
sometimes, but never life
With me, I bring to humanity
the only love and the only worthy life

Growing up, I was doomed
by things I found in the desert
My heart leaves unwanted knowledge
on doorknobs, pressing down, shut
In this world the raindrops never touch us at all
The raindrops kept safe in the clouds
forever
But if only you could have been
a childless mother

This is what I was told
by angels' ghosts, Mother
My heart is so far inside a crowded place
but I have no life
Circling around a circle

that's circling around a circle forever
the sun stole our center in the desert
Soft like a mother sheep
you spread yourself over all
all that you could ever imagine
with your mind shut

I strapped on a silver happiness
and walked into an empty room, shut
But you don't know
you don't know how little you mean to me, Mother
Tell me something that you know to be true
your heart beats, but it's not even in you at all
but it would be meaningless to wonder
how this would be if it were different if this were life

Growing up, I was doomed by things
that I found in the desert
and with me, I will keep these things forever
I am sinking in air forever
The death of the forgotten spread across the water
as uninvasive moonlight, our eyes shut
Even the dead can love better
than we can love in the desert

I always wished that I could place fingerprints
in places that were not crime scenes, Mother
With my body and my hands
I was grasping for air, your air, your life
You organize love and beauty
but love and beauty are not for all

I was not for all
and the part of me that was supposed to
endure all time forever
my love for humanity, is now the smallest

object in my hand, in this life
Every night, I look at it and wish that I were smaller
but it would never open; it is shut

and this love I have had for you
it has been the only love, Mother
but you have no knowledge of the things
that you left for me in the desert
a naked body, a dying tree
a grain of sand, a part of you
and still nothing at all

I am creating and ending people, shut
I want to be a part of the distance
I want to be the thing that looks at you
and says this is where you start
and this is where you end, Mother
And I want to be ok with the fact that
there was never and will never be
any life in the desert.

BLACK AND WHITE MEADOW

Looking at blood, you are colorblind
Looking at love, you see red

They say burning in Hell makes you feel something
but you do not believe in flames

As you are killing the daughter you love
she thanks you, instead

Now, you are lying
and everyone knows

After winter comes fall
then summer after that

Part 3

WARDROBE

ALL THE SUNSHINE

Meet me before the highway came
before we found the nest
in the chopped-down tree
before the grass was cut
and its dead limbs shut out
all the sunshine

Meet me before the gray
before the tsunami waves
swallowing teachers and daughters
Meet me that night they braided their hair
tanned skin and temporary tattoos

Meet me before our faces are
two-dimensional and recycled
gray
before our names are full of clues in a crossword
to the ending in which we ended

All the sunshine
and I will wait for you
with the shattered birds
and the blackened butterflies
in a dusty place by the window

MY ANCIENT ROBES OF LIFE

Thick, heavy, yet fragile
like ancient velvet fabric
is this life that covers me

I have always listened to the dryness
beyond the fountain

A rebellious nature
the very exception
of mathematical structures

I have always known
how easy it is
to tear apart

SMOKE AND MIRRORS

As the robe of velvet melts
an armor becomes visible
I slice my finger in half
on my own sword
pointing to the truth

With all things under the sun
your eyes cannot focus
on truths duality
I tear off my armor
set fire to my flesh
to cross another boundary
both atheistic and religiously
Where is humanity?

You think the sun beats the fire
They did not tell you of the smoke
In my insignificant suffering
I shall take all the world with me
into a uniform darkness

FORTRESS OF MEMORY

I am asleep from life
My sight turned pink and blue and black
I stared at the way out
until it turned to iron

OBSTACLE

I bought an iron shield
It broke in the mail
Can it still safeguard me
from the weak?

SOMETIMES

They say that women do not
have the ability to empty
their minds and think
of nothing. Well
sometimes, I
think of
you

UNDERGROUND

When you came from behind
to tighten the straps
on my backpack
I was not as small
as you thought I was

I cannot breathe now
and the heart cannot beat
The tunnel is black
but I finally see how
the future is greater than this

FOR FUCKS SAKE

You cry over losing your backpack
but there was nothing inside
There is no heaviness that you miss

BEFORE THE FLAYING

What if my skin is not my skin at all
but the skin of the world around me
protecting it
from whatever it is that I am?

INVERSION

I climbed to the top of the hill
without my eyes
and now the view looks at me

Part 4
WEDDING DRESS

THE WATERLILY AND THE FISHERMEN

Dressed in white
on the surface of a lake
perfectly still, I hold my head above water
in my wedding without guests

My beauty is tied down
to a bottom sprinkled with cadavers
So, I cut my chains
in search of the ocean

It is a gamble
It is race against time
to be seen before your flower fades
and the wildness takes hold

But what does beauty long for
except to be seen
and then to fade away?

THE MOUNTAIN

If you ever see this woman
the one standing on the tallest mountain
whose dress is longer than the mountain itself
that's when you'll know
that this day is her wedding day

To some of you
she might look like several different women
but those of us who know her
know that she is one and the same
The layer of clouds

you see at the very top
that is her veil
Her virginity is the snow
and now you must realize
she is not standing on the mountain anymore

This woman, she has become the mountain
she doesn't remember when
The taller trees are hidden well
there at the bottom
with the rest of all life
She does not move, but she does not linger

Some of you say she's never there at all
so much closer to the sun; but always colder
and all of you men freeze to death
before ever reaching her chest
That painful virginity of hers

your fingers blacken and fall off entirely
and you'll never touch anything again
Even if you risk your own life up there
to save many other men
in the end, none of you

can ever save her
but even more so, none of you will ever try
Here she has stood since the ice age
waiting for
a horizontal God.

CINDERELLA

Give me that midnight in between, I called
Give me that split second when the clock turns twelve
because all my life, black feathers have fallen from the sky
mocking me, taunting me
of whom I can't be and where I can't go

The prince misplaced all my moments, in sudden gravity
so that they became very hard to find- entirely
He loved me like my life was progress towards a greater good
He loved me like my life was progress
but all I craved was one split second of my own

Oh, my soul was the thing that buries you
Oh, my knowledge was the thing
the thing
that changes you from good to evil
I wanted that midnight

The story of Cinderella has taken on a grim new reality
The "hearts" of atoms are all in my hands
I devour prince after prince after prince after prince
in the search of a split second

and prince after prince after prince after prince
I get my Armageddon
when all that I ever wanted
was midnight
that midnight in between

EDGES

A daughter bruised
by early awakening
in a meadow-like swamp
filled with growing cotton
Her body moans by itself
with no mouth on her
Her arms are longer
and her nose drips clear liquid

There is something wrong with her
something that may or may not
always have been missing
She lifts the bone of her jaw

purely by the lightness of her soul
and all which was sunken
in thinned out muddy water
is now restored
Except, she forgot a mouth

and she made her arms too long
this morning
She is certain someone will notice
She is prepared to hear it
whatever it is you will tell her today

She will stir the foam in her cup
with a long, thin spoon
and look into its twisted mirror
Your golden words will fly
like angled butterflies
and all that matters in this world
will be the edge of you

Always, the days and the nights
eat away at all the best parts of her
like the white horse in the magazine
she saw when she was eleven
oh, she can't remember
what he looked like anymore

She has a purpose because
the hollow parts of her
are all sexual features
They confirm that everyone else
is bigger, greater, and more solid than she

Every dream she dreams
and every nightmare
is a mathematical equation
of what she used to look like
so she will remember it the next day
and wake up looking like what she used to

The white tips of her black eyelashes
they burn away before anyone notices
they were ever there
as the sunrise and sunset conjoin
and unite and conform
into the same religion

Will you take the hands
of this unclothed wasteland
and remember the laughter
shaped like the idea of a star
shaped like the idea of a heart
these unreachable
and unattainable edges

which could flip her around
and make her walk
into her own body
like it was something natural
That laughter — an echo, a signal

red tongues
and perfectly comfortable heels, edges
the white in their eyes glittering
as they stare rudely
into their own futures
so sharp and traceable
their eyelashes will never dissolve like hers
like the cold metal needles
sinking into their lips
on certain Fridays

Your body
like a drunken sleepwalking zombie giant
you make your way through the air
with those flickering shadows
waving like a princess in captive
behind you on the wall

She pours melted caramel into her flesh
and becomes a bit younger
She twists and turns naked in the mud
like she is bedridden with a strong fever
and she remembers why
she made her arms longer this day

DENIAL AND ISOLATION

I am sinking into a bathtub
that may very well
be the oldest object in the world
It was here before us
it is stained with the relief stripes
of blue paint that at some point dripped
down on it from above
above, where the walls are white
where they have always been white

A smile can push empty boxes sideways
until the very edge
make them disappear
but they will demonstrate their only weight
their surface, heavy enough to make them fall
in the end — a soulless box

Yesterday I had perfect skin
and a perfect set of eyes
I had shaped my eyes
with fluoroantimonic acid
I had lengthened my arms
with a stretching torture rack
I was elevating three centimeters
above the ground
That is when you told me

that something was hiding inside my body
You told me that it was me
and you told me what that was
You said I was a kind person
because I often cried

You are gone most of the time, aren't you?
Aren't you jumping around in the woods
pretending to be a bunny rabbit?
Aren't you extracting the healing powers
from the forest fairies?

Aren't you building
the tallest building in the world
in the middle of the deepest part of the ocean?
Aren't you dead most of the time? Aren't you?
Aren't you important?
Aren't you always right?

Look, there are flowers on the table
I got them myself
took them off your gravestone at the graveyard
(It wasn't me: Who put it there?)
I know the flowers don't look right anymore
All the time they were here waiting

THE UNLIKELY MEMORIES

I opened fifteen chambers in my heart
greatest exhibition in all of Arabia
I filled them with live lobsters
and in my head, I imagined them all red

The truth is they were always gray
and my blood was the red parts
and they lived in a crippling fear of the color red
These lobsters — they prayed things into existence

Only they knew the true nature of the Gods
Only they knew them
I would have these unlikely memories of deep-water life
I'd be drenched in sweat every night, starving

I swallowed a dryness that was so specific
as if described by someone's first encounter
with dryness
like the geometrical cut of a diamond

I will never forget the political demonstration
taking place in the same public square
in which I had dreamt of your murder
You pulled me and dragged me through oceans of protesters

My sister said she could see our love
but how did it look?
Maybe like a long train of red silk
dragged through all the rooms of a Shanghai building

Seemingly liquid and consenting
this incredible dryness and unpleasant texture

and just a step of a shoe could have caught it
It was never anything beyond human

You incorporated it into your dressing
into a tie that never came undone
James Bond, you casually slid down a floor (which had become vertical)
I felt some type of insanity

I was not its slave, but it was mine
It was not an experience, but a feeling
and whether I am autistic or psychopathic
cannot ever begin to explain

something which can be felt
but not experienced
as if every moment stands on its very own
and can never be tied together

I am paralyzed by a silence
although I am not deaf
and there is certainly music
There is always music.

TO WASTE IT ALL

The dream I had last night only consisted of
sleeping while you were watching me
This once seemed like an achievable dream
I thought I could travel wherever whenever
and still feel your warm presence

I think that it is true
that I have needed saving from our relationship
for quite some time
I guess I always thought it would be you
who saved me

You probably believe that I want all these other things
that I want to be with an artist
explore my sexuality
have a spontaneous and adventurous life
and end up with many children

But you should know
that those are only things that I should want
if I were in my right mind
if I took my own life seriously
but no

What I want is to waste it all
for you
to dream all my life of the things I gave up
and have you standing by my bed
adjusting my blanket

What I want is to die inside your kindness
and never wake up to a world

where that kindness has been
the only thing that was ever
wasted

I know in my heart
that you won't be able to hold on to it
if I wake up
I know you'll never be kind again
I know

I'll chase you after that
and I know that when I find you again
you will be forced to kill me
You will have to drown me
in a long glass tube filled with water

a simple decorative installment
at a French movie premiere
and all these artists I could have known
there on their date nights, will stop and stare
They will always go to French movie premieres after that

trying to find back to that moment
when all the truths of the world
unfolded in front of their very eyes
Was it real? Was it expensive? Was it
planned down to every detail

or partially improvised along the way?
I'd rather die slowly like this
with no one questioning your actions, my actions
with thick, black curtains and no one ever seeing
my face or what I gave away to keep you

But sadly, they are breaking in
and they all seem to think

that you shouldn't have set our house on fire
although you and I, we both know
you should have.

NO DOGS IN THE DOORWAY

Continuously getting cleaner and more saint-like
until her very skin melts off her bones
and slips into a jewelry box
her breasts and backsides attached to it
revealing no flesh or fat ever existed
nor was it needed
to hold up her construction

but only the very birth her mother once had given
and through that a careful illusion
and a loud snap
Who is going to leave her family's legacy
flayed skin on your countertop
behind the books she bought you

leathercovered words and she knows
you'll never find it there
the jewelry box
The answer is no one
All of this is a lie
every word she is saying
every word she ever said

There are no dogs in the doorway
These bones are not enough for them
These dogs are not enough for her
crushing her remains
Maybe the only thing that is ever true

is how deep the child lies within us
All her bones shall go to the wrong species
and the cannibals shall be howling

their backs not straight anymore
only their sexual orientation
but not the greed

But luckily for you, you'd never risk that
you'd never risk accidentally seeing her
before she's utterly gone from here, anywhere
She was never here
There are no dogs in the doorway.

PARASITICAL SYMBIOSIS

One time, in the middle of a joke
and completely by accident
you spotted my emotions between the trees
in the form of a carnivore
as we were crossing the border
from Norway to Sweden

and the hunter in you confronted the ecologist
As a hunter, you'd take down your opponents
you'd kill all the carnivores
lie back and watch innocent life
blossom again
so you could kill that, too

You pulled out all this information about me
it is beyond annoying
these extra lives I've had to offer you

these men I've always had to give away
You don't even know how to take advantage of them
like I do
and, to be honest I feel it is a waste

to have you lurking behind the bushes with your rifle
I have almost been faithful to you
except those four times, only those fifty times
maybe that's a lie, but I can't remember numbers

I'm a wolf, and I guess you'd never believe this
but my favorite flowers are black roses
and I don't respond well to cold hearts
How can you hold me responsible?

for the things that YOU don't understand?
You're not even wild
all you supposedly have is this large brain
you are a hunter, and you have a choice

My intelligent superior
you can spare me
you can only observe me like this
my true nature — you can learn to know me better

but you will eat me whole, you will
worms and all I have
and maybe rabies, maybe
and these bullets — you will eat these

You will digest all of this without any issues
but my face — you'll hang it on the wall with glass eyes
and there will be no souls in there
In that house, there won't be any

SEASHELL

The hollow labyrinth
the short-spanned loyalty
stretching unnaturally into a spiral
slowly and painfully
like a squirming worm
trying to avoid running into

a pointy and definite end
I am a breathing being
holding, cradling an emptiness
as my only prized possession
sounds like waves in the ocean
sounds like a calling, a longing

Don't you lose it all
behind my pearly whites
Don't you get lost in
all this wide, thick
nothing

At the swollen stage
of decomposition
my fragile, thin shell
cracks
My eyes of glass are shattering

My fluids are leaking
like a rainbow-colored slinky
down the stairs
This little game
we played
in my childbearing years

was much like death to me
but think of me
on the sunny days
by the emergency exits.

TIDELESS

These sweet suitors, they make me smile
They make me happy; they make me care for them
They are like plus signs
like birds with the water as pearls on their white feathers

This love is too big, and so, with you I drown
in the hopelessness of it all
Every time I think to myself to try to be open
to let you hug me without crossing my arms over my body
without pushing you away

Why do I want to protect every stranger
hug them and rub their arms when they get cold?
But with you, if you were bleeding in the streets
I feel like I still wouldn't be able to
reach out of my paralysis

to cry for help, to cry
to keep my eyes open
to even wake up
There you would lie, and I'd turn my head
and my shorter haircut would not give me any trouble

in this wind
It is not as perfect as it should have been
and I can't stand that
I am just lingering here missing all opportunities for intimacy
or attention, or even the slightest bit of mercy

I just can't give it to you
I cut my hair, and I am trying to float while asleep
There is no salt in the water

but there are sharks
"What kind of place is this?"

That is the question I ask myself
feeling the life of this relationship slowly being spent
I'm waiting, eagerly waiting, sweating
the hairs standing up on my arms
Even under an open sky
I am trapped in our house

My toes are getting tired from gripping the floor
Ready to pounce, I am fully dressed
My hair is long again
My face is younger
The only thing that must happen is
to wake up from this coma

and forget the last couple of years
so that I can be alive with you again
so that I can love you again
and we can be free
The only thing that was ever true

was my love for you
and my traumatic experiences, they actually
never happened
yet this icy snowball keeps snowballing
getting bigger and bigger

You ask me all these questions
My answers come out through the vent
like gas in a gas chamber
and I don't really know why
my guilt is nowhere to be found:

why it is not retrievable

I might be playing poker and not even know it
myself
Are my cards on the table?
How many times did I already break up

with you?
The stones:
I throw mine as far as I can into the water
but you keep yours
All the bugs right there on the surface:

the fish, they come up to kill them off
devour them hole
in a random pattern
What? What am I trying to say?
What? What am I trying to feel?

There is a frog that saves me
the second frog I've seen since we first moved
to this country
The frog, it makes me smile, it makes me cry
This frog, I can look at it forever

We stand under the tree
until it is so soaked in rainwater
that it makes us even wetter than being under
an open sky
and in our house, there is nothing that can save us

UNDYING

This is not four corners
not a home for you
The corner, the single corner
that's the one with the everchanging view

You don't see the sky
the fact that nothing stops
All you see is me
You don't see the rush

in a speedy and windless free fall
of thousands of suicides
a stream of silver fish
they seem faster together

Oh, the snowflakes
you just see the one
as it keeps falling
so pale are the ashes

from the sun
Such a long time it takes
for the innocent to fall
I am the tint

of the space
to the furthest mountain
that mountain
which used to be

your wife
I am the eternally long time

it takes for something to diminish
and turn slightly blue

slightly colder
slightly less true
not time
nor death

but only the rooftops
stop the stars
from reaching
you

don't see the sky —

ORANGE

Do you remember how plastic chairs
have saved us in the past? When you
are too tired to stand but too happy
to want to sleep forever — that magical
state of mind when the world spreads
and prolongs into vulgar and useless
inventions, keeping you alive

We had the same blood type
same almond-shaped eyes
I stood under the energy towers
waited for leukemia that never came
You took my hand, led me into the olive fields
I felt the sand coming into my mouth
and did not mind the taste

You picked up some rocks
in case the wild dogs came
told me to watch out for the town drunks
Throughout the years, you have lent me
your sleep, and I have lent you mine
and each time I fell asleep
you'd greet me with a smile

But my parents taught me
knots are stronger than bows
and if I could have loved me in your place
I would have spared you from it

And that plastic factory right next to your house
and that smell of plastic
back when we cared so much about our health

and always wore red and orange clothes
accepting our own beauty, hell, almost endorsed it
now the dirty orange color
from the pollution in the sky
reminds me of that
now that our beauty is choking us

But maybe all good things I ever did
and all the bad things I never did
were because I like the way my name
is written in their suicide letters
like the only truly honest moment of their lives
was when these men loved me despite everything

And is that so bad? Is that so cruel
that maybe I have wanted to see
how they would describe me then
how they would know me then
if they ever knew me
But if I could have loved me in their place
I would have spared them from it

Part 5
WHEN COLOR FOLDS

CORNER MOON

This side is smooth and rounded
This side keeps us tilting forward
The other side has two edges
and a gaping hole in between
That is our moon
that we drew in the corner of the sky

THE FOLD

A plastic ball filled with air
separating the boats and the swimmers
and no one knows what my face looks like in there
No one knows if I am smiling
or if I am really and truly dead

I know I am not the only one laughing
Sometimes I dig so deep beneath the ground
that the sky can't remain where it is
It starts folding together in the middle
where I am bending down

All the birds, all the planes
all the clouds, the stars, moon, and sun
they start rushing sliding to the middle and down
into that fold of the sky
and so, all the things

are pouring into this grave now
lower than Hell but not too low
and to that place where I go
so will the entire sky follow
into the dark blue

BAD CHOICES

Yellow mindsets
false days
Christmas ornaments
in the rain
a full moon
that is anything but round

Oh, I look for the light
anywhere I can
Your white thoughts
and your superiority
in a yellow world
you shine even brighter

So, I'm sticking to you
like bad choices
and
someone else's
beer
in the fluorescent lights

a moth and its ugly wings
its alarming potential
to fly away
to whatever reveals itself
to be
even brighter

BLACK

Is this a serious moment?
That is the question in your mind
The smallest butterfly flies
in front of the sun
and all our memories turn black

SNARVEI

Du er redd for å[set ring over a] fly
og få[set ring over a]r ikke besøkt de du elsker
Du tror du kan dø av det
«Det er bare tull» sier jeg
«Husk OL hå[set ring over a]pet som døde
av lynnedslag fra en klar himmel»
Du kan ikke unngå[set ring over a] kjærligheten

Så[set ring over a] du legger nøklene dine i fryseren
tenker ikke lenger
fordi det er så[set ring over a] mye å[set ring over a] tenke på[set ring over a]
Snart, har du så[set ring over a] då[set ring over a]rlig tid
at du begynner å[set ring over a] løpe
før du vet veien
Dit hvor flyet skulle reist

kommer du aldri
Jeg skulle ønske at noen hadde hardnet hjertet ditt
før du havnet her hvor alt gå[set ring over a]r i oppløsning
Jeg skulle ønske at du hadde lært å[set ring over a] elske
litt etter litt
ikke alt på[set ring over a] en gang

at du ikke døde på[set ring over a] grunn av et øyeblikk
som kunne ha skjedd hvem som helst
Fargen av himmelen
fører meg ikke til deg
Må[set ring over a]nen er kun for oss som er igjen

og den er forræderisk

SHORTCUT

You are scared to fly
and do not visit those you love
You think you can die from it
"It's just nonsense," I say
"Remember the Olympic talent
who died of lightning from a clear sky"
You cannot escape love

So, you put your keys in the freezer
no longer thinking
because there is so much to think about
Soon, you are in such a hurry
that you start running
before you know where you are running to

The plane is landing
but you will never arrive
I wish someone had hardened your heart
before you went where everything falls apart
I wish you had learned to love
little by little

not all at once
that you did not die because of one moment
that could have happened to anyone
The color of the sky
does not lead me to you
The moon is only for us who are left

and it is treacherous

THE WAVE

There is a naked thought
in a place where no other thoughts can be found
It is a thought about change

That very moment this particular change will occur
that is when the thought will be gone forever
and in its place will be a girl

Yes, there is a girl waving
on the other side of the ocean
She is wearing stud earrings

They are not real diamonds
but that's ok because she's not a real person
Tomorrow morning, I'll have a cup of coffee

and then I will swim over there
to the waving girl with the stud earrings
and the objective perspective

which we all have been searching for
I can tell she is down to earth
and less demanding than I

I suppose those small puddles
from when the ocean was fuller
I suppose those puddles will still be there

when I get back
but if you see them disappearing
into the ocean again

then you'll know that you have to
let me go
because, in that case

the ocean, even in its absolute smallest form
even that was too big for this one thought
and the girl could never make it

PROMISE

I unfolded the summers
that you promised
They were empty

GULLABLE

You have the color of a seagull
the dirtiest white
what an offensive innocence

ROPE

You won't let me fall
but you will let me hang

Part 6
THE FIRST RIPPLE

MY FUNNY VALENTINE

The Devil drags me through all the water
and all the Earth
with his beautiful face pressed against mine
and it is a kind of hurtful beauty

He drags me through all the pain
and all the nothingness
until he puts me back on a fishing boat
in the middle of the ocean
at the mercy of simple fishermen

I look up at them, all average looking
and I reject salvation

MACHINE GUN CONFUSION

The shapes are that of two people
They do each have a soul
but it's hard for them to remember who they are
when they constantly get new bodies
and brains filled with memories

Some of these brains lack certain qualities
like proper impulse processing
or the ability to produce oxytocin
Sometimes these beings look down and find
that they have machine guns in their human hands

Every time my prison cell opens
and these two prison guards come through the door
they have a disgusting and awkward look of displacement
a look of being forced to live as someone else
wondering what is the essence of a soul?

WHAT IF THE CLOUDS ARE A FOG?

Once,
God was a teenage boy full of pimples
He sat next to me on the stone
of an empty fountain structure
There he leaned close to me
with his hand in my crotch
The worst thing was how he stared
into my eyes while doing it

In fact,
I could not hear him when
he told me all the secrets of the world
I was too preoccupied with how
unattractive he was to me
Was I being too judgmental? Too arrogant?
Did I have too many human limitations?
Was God trying to tell me
that I can be the smartest person in the world

and ask all the right questions
but unless I accept rape from a minor
the answer will continue
to stare me dead in the eyes
and I won't be able to see it?

BRAND NEW HEAVEN

I tried to accept everything
so that I could come to Heaven
but when I got there
heaven was closed with cement
The limbs of angels were hanging from it
lifeless and swollen
I guess they are doing construction
changing the whole thing now
so that all my sacrifice in life
was for nothing
Who knows what the new Heaven will be like?

NO TITLE

What about a god
who likes nothing about herself?
Where can she hide?

POINT

The heavier you are, the steadier
I will sink you to the bottom
so you can perfect your aim

VACATION FROM DESTINY

I don't think the water around us is water at all
with its total stillness
and floating objects that normally would sink

It is clear to me now
that we, somewhere along the last twenty years
tricked destiny and changed the world

so that nothing could sink anymore

PINOCCHIO

You are right there in his head
The way you become a demon
is by telling him that he is delusional
You become an archangel
by believing in him

JOKE

Without language, I would not understand
you
Without language, I would know
myself

So let us build
skyscrapers for the birds
Take these fourteen deaths and one life
and start again
with words

LIGHT

So, there you stand
with your flickering light
wishing you were
there

FOURTH DIMENSION

Dancing is visible time
Music is auditory time
Orientation is time multiplied
Love is the opposite of time

www.ingramcontent.com/pod-product-compliance
Lightning Source LLC
Chambersburg PA
CBHW071712040426
42446CB00011B/2030